SO-BFA-216

Interactive
Bulletin Boards
LANGUAGE ARTS

By
Judy Meagher
and
Joan Novelli

SCHOLASTIC
PROFESSIONAL BOOKS

NEW YORK • TORONTO • LONDON • AUCKLAND • SYDNEY

ACKNOWLEDGMENTS

Heartfelt thanks to Deborah Schecter, our editor at Scholastic Professional Books, for her artful guidance. Special thanks, also, to Paula Butterfield and the Bozeman School District; the teachers at Emily Dickinson School, Whittier School, Morning Star, and Heritage Christian School in Bozeman, Montana, for their help, support, and cooperation; and to all the children who brought the bulletin boards pictured in this book to life.

Scholastic Inc. grants teachers permission to photocopy the designated reproducible pages from this book for classroom use. No other part of this publication may be reproduced in whole or in part, or stored in a retrieval system, or transmitted in any form or by any means, electronic, mechanical, photocopying, recording, or otherwise, without written permission of the publisher. For information regarding permission, write to Scholastic Inc., 555 Broadway, New York, NY 10012.

Project direction by Joan Novelli
Cover design by Jaime Lucero
Cover art by Jo Lynn Alcorn
Cover photographs by Judy Meagher
Interior design by Solutions by Design, Inc.
Interior photographs by Judy Meagher
Interior illustration by Paige Billin-Frye, except page 22 by Abby Carter

ISBN 0-590-21235-4

Copyright © 1998 by Judy Meagher and Joan Novelli

All rights reserved. Printed in the U.S.A.

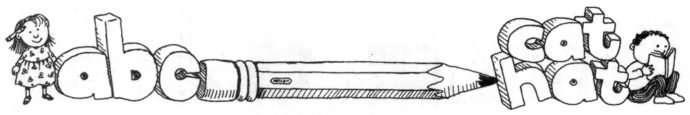

Contents

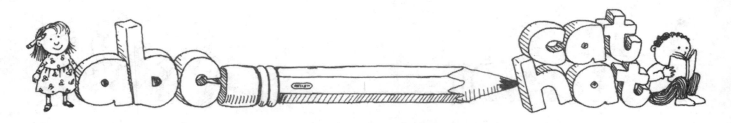

From the Authors

When it comes to putting up bulletin boards, are you a little reluctant? As beginning teachers, we both remember approaching bulletin boards with some discomfort. We wondered how we could create the wonderful-looking boards we envisioned and how we would do it all by ourselves. Then there was the expectation that they would require constant change and attention.

Bulletin boards can be an intimidating part of teaching. You worry about being neat and creative. You wonder how many more letters you can cut out and what to do about a border. And then there's always what goes on the board and why. Student work? Something seasonal?

Rather than let your boards be ruled by changing seasons and approaching holidays (often unwelcome signs that it's time for a new board), think instead of bulletin boards that change and grow with your students, engaging them right from the start. These interactive boards do more than brighten your classroom walls. They become teaching tools, enriching your learning environment and involving students every step of the way—from titles and borders to everything in between.

This book is designed to guide you and your students in creating exciting interactive boards that will support your language arts curriculum. From beginning-of-the-year boards that build a sense of class community to publishing centers, story stacks, seasonal story walls, sequencing stations, and more, the teacher- and child-tested bulletin boards in this book celebrate children's learning, each creating a friendly hub of activity that will bring children back again and again. Here's a look at what a board like this can do:

◉ **All About Us** (see page 9): Start the year with a board that invites children to build houses, using words and pictures to tell about themselves, their

families, and so on. As they add on to their stories over time, their houses will grow. Children will love landscaping the board too, adding trees, flowers, roads, cars, whatever they like. A board like this helps children feel immediately at home in a new classroom. It also encourages them to get to know one another and gives you an early indication of literacy levels.

◉ **Take a Memo!** (see page 36): Turn a bulletin board into a giant memo board to give children real-life reasons to read and write every day.

◉ **Bag a Story** (see page 62): Paper bags attached to a board contain pictures and ideas that will inspire stories and teach elements of writing, including character, setting, and conflict.

⊙ **Poetry Place** (see page 30): Make poetry a part of every day with a board that features words and phrases from favorite poems that children can put together to create new poems. The words and phrases are written on sentence strips trimmed to size, making it easy for children to play with them and put them together as they wish.

What's Inside

Like these examples, the other boards in this book are designed to grow and change over time, relieving you of the time-consuming task of putting up new boards each month and allowing children the time they need to participate in meaningful ways. For each of the 24 boards featured in this book, you'll find:

⊙ **Photographs:** To guide you and your students in building each board, photos indicate what the displays look like in real classrooms. As your students interact with their boards, they'll put their own stamp on them.

⊙ **Learning Links:** Each board can support your curriculum in numerous ways. This section suggests a few possibilities.

⊙ **Border Box:** This section offers suggestions for easy ways to tailor-make eye-catching borders for each board.

⊙ **Materials:** Everything you need to make your boards is included in a list of easy-to-find and generally inexpensive materials. (See Help From Home.)

HELP FROM HOME

Part of what makes bulletin boards appealing is the splash of color they add to a classroom. From the background paper that covers the board to the markers students use for various activities, having bright, fresh materials on hand is a plus. To keep your classroom well stocked, consider inviting parents to donate an item or two at the beginning and middle of the year. Craft paper in assorted colors, nonfading construction paper, assorted markers and other writing and coloring tools, straight pins, pushpins, adding machine tape (for borders), plus a bunch of small boxes and other containers (see Handy Holders, page 6) are some of the materials you might request.

⊙ **Steps:** From putting down background paper to adding finishing touches, this section guides you in getting your boards going.

⊙ **Variations:** Sometimes a bulletin board lends itself to variations—for example, changes to suit younger or older students. The ideas here offer some options.

⊙ **Teaching With the Board:** Here you'll find activities that take each bulletin board further, including literature links, math and science spin-offs, language arts mini-lessons, and more.

⊙ **Reproducible Pages:** From templates to journal pages, these reproducibles are ready to use with your students. Keep their interests and needs in mind as you use these pages. Rather than limit children to what is on the reproducibles, use them as a starting place and see what students have to add.

Handy Holders

Having tools right where they need them offers children a welcoming invitation to visit the board and take part. Here are a few how-to's for making handy holders.

Pin envelopes of all sizes and colors to a board to hold papers, graph markers, and other materials.

Roll the top down on a paper bag. Pin or staple it to the board, or punch a hole and hang it from a pushpin.

Boxes of all shapes and sizes, including milk cartons, make great holders. Punch a couple of holes and hang from straight pins. If you want the contents to show, cut a window out of the box and tape a piece of acetate to the inside.

Hang felt pens in their original boxes. Empty the pens, use pushpins or staples to secure the box from the inside, then restock.

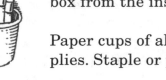

Paper cups of all sizes hold markers, scissors, and other supplies. Staple or punch a hole and hang from a straight pin.

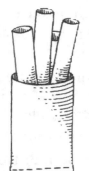

Roll cardboard or sturdy paper and staple one end flat to hold paper and other supplies.

To make see-through pockets to hold numerous pairs of scissors, stitch or staple acetate at regular intervals to a strip of cardboard. You can do the same thing with resealable sandwich bags, stapling several to a strip of cardboard.

Fruit baskets make colorful holders. Use pushpins to attach to your board.

Use tagboard strips to make pockets for holding just about anything.

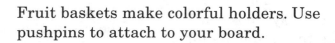

For a change, tack up clothesline and use clothespins to hang materials such as graph markers or small paperback books. Dangle the clothesline to clip materials vertically.

Bright Borders

Brighten displays by inviting students to help create one-of-a-kind borders. Often a bulletin board topic will suggest an idea. For example, children's self-portraits are just right for displays about themselves. (See All About Us, page 9.) For an appealing border you can adapt for many boards, see Accordion Fold Borders, below.

For even more inspiration, start up a classroom Border Company—a bulletin board for creating student-designed borders for your class and others. This "think tank" has great potential as a learning tool (ties in language arts, math, problem-solving, and more) and self-esteem booster. Count on it being one of your students' favorite places to spend time!

Steps

Materials

⊙ assorted paper supplies

⊙ pushpins

⊙ markers

⊙ border order form

1 Section off an end of a chalkboard or wall. Have children cover it with butcher paper and add a heading that says "The Border Company." Stock a nearby worktable with markers and other materials students might like to use.

2 Together, create a border order form. (See page 8.) Make copies and store in a folder or clipboard near the display.

3 Brainstorm kinds of borders. If possible, take a tour of other classrooms to see a variety of borders. (Bring clipboards to take notes.) List ideas. Let children fill out a border order form for practice, using one of the ideas. Review length of border strips, descriptions, and so on.

4 Guide children in making a few border samples, each about three feet long to show any repeating patterns. Display these with labels at the Border Company board.

5 Have children take border orders for other classrooms and design them.

ACCORDION-FOLD BORDERS

You can adapt the pattern shown here to make just about any kind of repeating pattern for a bulletin board border. Make sure that children leave a section on both the left and right uncut as shown. (Otherwise the pages will come apart instead of staying attached.)

Scholastic Professional Books, 1998

Name _____ Date _____

The Border Company

BORDER ORDER FORM

Name of Client _____

Date_____

Bulletin Board Subject _____

Border Description_____

_____

_____

To Do

Sample Border Only _____

Full Border _____

Border Size

Top _____

Bottom _____

Left Side _____

Right Side_____

Other _____

Total Length of Finished Border _____

Date Needed By _____

Comments _____

_____

_____

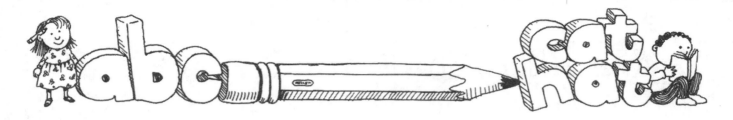

All About Us

Begin the year with a board that lets students get to know one another and gives you a jump on building a spirit of community in your classroom. Variations are included to show the many forms this board can take. (See page 10.) Use your board with the reproducible (see page 12) to encourage even more interaction.

BORDER BOX
Borders that work well for this board include handprints, student-drawn faces, and pictures of a variety of homes.

TIP
Plan ahead for this activity by asking parents to send in photographs of family members, their children engaged in favorite activities, and so on. In class, allow students to build their houses for this board over a period of days, adding information about themselves and their families. Consider setting up a workstation stocked with blank paper and other supplies near this board so that students can add on to their houses when they wish.

LANGUAGE ARTS LINKS
Students write or dictate words and sentences about themselves and then read others' work to find out how they are like and different from their classmates.

Building the Board

Steps

1 Make and display a headline that says "All About Us." A wall space (in the classroom or hallway) works well for this display.

2 Brainstorm and list information students can share about themselves, such as where they live, the people in their families, activities they enjoy, and so on. Have them use the 10- by 10-inch paper to write about and draw pictures of any of the items on the list. (Or, if you prefer, choose several items and guide students in completing information for each one.)

3 Cut blank paper in half diagonally to make roofs. Have children each write their name on a roof and decorate. Then let them take turns at the display, building their homes by starting with the roof and then adding on stories. (Each level is a whole sheet of paper.) Suggest that children leave plenty of space at the bottom to add on.

4 When children have completed their homes, they can landscape the display, adding pictures of trees, flowers, streetlights, pets, and more.

Materials

⊙ paper (cut into 10- by 10-inch squares)
⊙ markers
⊙ photos (optional)
⊙ scissors
⊙ tape

Variations

Inside Our Homes:
Let children use butcher or craft paper to cut out the shapes of their homes. Then ask them to divide the homes into rooms and use pictures and words to tell about themselves—for example, describing what they do in each room.

A Skyful of Students:
Students decorate and string paper-plate raindrops from clouds to create this display. Begin by having children cut out cloud shapes from craft paper. Have them write their names on the clouds and decorate. Help children punch several holes near the bottom

10

of their clouds and string lengths of yarn through each. Have them punch holes in raindrop-shaped pieces of paper, tie each one to a piece of yarn, and use the drops to draw pictures and write words about themselves.

Teaching With the Board

To create a sense of class community at the beginning of the year—or any other time you want to pull students together—try these activities.

Ways We're Alike: Encourage students to find out more about similarities and differences among classmates with the reproducible on page 12. Ask students to begin by filling in information about themselves. Have them add a category of their own choosing too. Next, let them talk to one another to find classmates with similarities in each category. Have children sign one another's papers to show what they have in common. (More than one student may sign for each category.)

Great Glyphs: A glyph (short for hieroglyphic) is a picture that conveys information. Let children make glyphs to tell about themselves. Begin by making a legend together. Decide what shapes and/or colors will represent different interests, ages, and so on. The example here shows a simple one to start with.

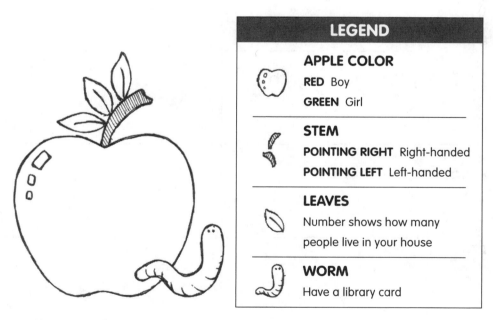

LEGEND
APPLE COLOR
RED Boy
GREEN Girl
STEM
POINTING RIGHT Right-handed
POINTING LEFT Left-handed
LEAVES
Number shows how many people live in your house
WORM
Have a library card

Adapted from *Super Graphs, Venns & Glyphs* by Honi Bamberger and Patricia Hughes (Scholastic Professional Books, 1995). Used by permission of the publisher.

All About Us

Fill in the information under "Me." For each number, find at least one classmate with the same answer. Have each person sign your sheet.

	Me	**A Classmate**
1. Eye Color		
2. Number of People in My Family		
3. Favorite Activity		
4. Something I Do Well		
5. My Birthday Month		
6. Favorite Food		
7.		

INTERACTIVE BULLETIN BOARDS • LANGUAGE ARTS
Scholastic Professional Books, 1998

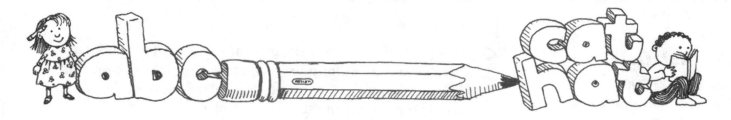

Linking Letters

This bright board invites young children to build letters and words using tagboard cut into strips and shapes.

BORDER BOX
Let children write letters of the alphabet on border-width strips and put them together to make a border. The character on this board was made by cutting shapes from paper and putting them together with brads. Children can manipulate the character to move arms, legs, and so on.

LANGUAGE ARTS LINKS

Children are naturally drawn to tactile experiences. This board builds on that interest to encourage language development—from recognizing letter shapes to building and reading words.

Building the Board

Steps

1   Cover the board with craft paper and hang a sign that says "Linking Letters." If you're feeling ambitious, make this sign out of handmade letters formed with shapes and connected with brads (just as children will form their own letters). Otherwise, just write it on a strip of contrasting-color craft paper.

Materials

- ⊙ craft paper
- ⊙ posterboard, assorted colors
- ⊙ scissors
- ⊙ straight pins
- ⊙ brads

2 Cut posterboard into shapes that can be used to form letters. You'll need long and short rectangles, circles, and horseshoe shapes. To make the letters shown on page 13, use the measurements shown here.

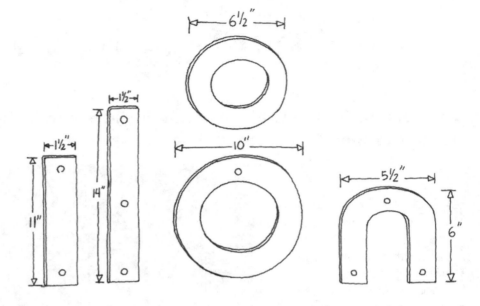

3 Punch a hole in the appropriate place on each shape where children will join the shapes to make letters. (See illustration.)

4 Tack up a small sign at the bottom left or right that says "Brads." Attach the brad box beneath the sign. (See page 6 for directions on adding boxes to bulletin boards.)

5 Use straight pins to hang shapes on the board, grouping like-shapes together.

6 Demonstrate how to use a brad to link two shapes. Then let children take over, selecting shapes, sizes, and brads to make their own letters. (This is a good floor activity, though you can set up a worktable nearby too.)

TIP

As children use the shapes to form letters, they may want to put letters together to build words. You can help emerging writers who can identify the initial letter of a word by helping them sound out the final letter. Beginning and ending sounds are typically easier to recognize than those in the middle.

14

Teaching With the Board

Children will have plenty of fun using this board for free play. If you want to direct their letter-making to support skills you're teaching, try these extensions:

Spell It: Write part of a word on a piece of paper, leaving blanks for children to complete. Pin the word to the board and let them use the shapes to form complete words.

Word Play: Let children make more letter connections with this word-building game. Divide a sheet of copy paper into 24 squares—four across, six down—and duplicate. Have children play in pairs, taking turns writing a letter in a square. How many words can they build on one page? (Like Scrabble, words can intersect.)

Rhyming Rows: At the board, feature a word representing a phonogram (or word family) you are teaching. Have children use the letter shapes to build words in this word family. For example, feature the word *jet* and let children experiment with building other words with the *et* phonogram. Set up a pocket chart activity near the board to reinforce the experience. Write the starter word on a sentence strip and highlight the letters *et* for easy identification. Add a picture for a visual clue. Have children write words that go in this family on sentence strips, illustrate them (or paste on pictures they cut out), trim to size, and place them in pockets next to the starter word. Add new word families to the chart to create rows of rhyming words.

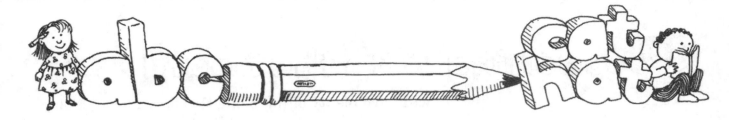

Flashlight Fun

Children's fascination with flashlights will draw them to this board, where they'll build sentences by shining the light on words in different categories.

BORDER BOX

The picture here shows a border of multicolored strips along with an inner border of flashlights. Children can make a similar border by cutting flashlights from construction paper and using them to frame the board.

LANGUAGE ARTS LINKS

This board lets children build both silly and sensible sentences, expanding their vocabulary with the words on the board and increasing their awareness of the mechanics of writing.

Building the Board

Steps

1 Cover a board with blue craft paper. Have children use construction paper to make a border of flashlights. Add a heading that says "Flashlight Fun." Beneath this, add a sentence that says "Add words and shine on some sentences!"

2 Tack up yellow paper inside the flashlight border. (Leave 10 to 12 inches of blue showing.)

Materials

- craft paper (blue, white, yellow)
- construction paper
- scissors
- mini-flashlights
- baskets or boxes
- string, sturdy tape
- pushpins
- large flashlight
- clipboards
- black marker

TIP

You may want to start the board with just three columns of words—beginnings, middles, and endings. For children who aren't ready to add their own words to the board, you can take dictation, writing down words they suggest.

3 Add real flashlights to the board. Place them in baskets or open boxes (see page 6 for directions). If you're using key-ring flashlights, you can use pushpins to hang them up.

You can also tie string around the bottom of small flashlights, secure with sturdy tape, then hang from pushpins. Lean a large flashlight against the board (or place nearby). Add a couple of clipboards so that children can record the sentences they make.

4 Use a black marker to divide the yellow paper into columns, one each for nouns, verbs, prepositions, and articles. Add a few words in each column yourself, then demonstrate how to shine the flashlight on different words to form a sentence.

5 Let children take over, adding words to each column and shining on sentences, one word at a time.

Teaching With the Board

You can easily adapt this board to support what's going on in your classroom. Some suggestions follow.

Categories: Use the board to support other areas of learning. For example, select words that relate to animals, seasons, space, sports, or any other theme children are studying.

Buddy Work: Encourage students to work together, one shining the light to make sentences while the other records the words. Students can switch places so that each gets a turn with the flashlight—and each takes a turn putting the words together on paper to form a sentence.

Sentence-Strip Scramble: Provide sentence strips for students to record their sentences. Have them cut them up (one or more words per piece) and place the pieces in an envelope. Pin a box to the board to hold these scrambled sentences. Challenge children to put the pieces in each envelope together to make a sentence. Have children sign their names to each envelope they complete.

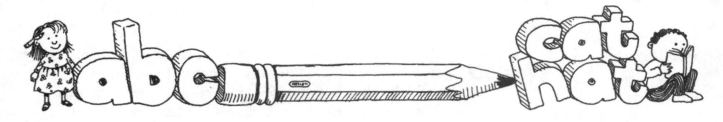

Sentence Scramble

Children use sticky notes to unscramble sentences on this giant game board. You can get the board going with a few sentences of your own. Students will eagerly take over, putting up their own sentences to tell scrambled stories.

BORDER BOX

Write one giant scrambled sentence (or a couple) on sentence strips to create an interactive border. Children can replace the border periodically with their own scrambled sentence strips.

LANGUAGE ARTS LINKS

This board helps children focus on letters and words as they relate to one another in a sentence.

Building the Board

Steps

1 Cover a board with craft paper. Add a heading that says "Unscramble the Sentences."

2 Write scrambled sentences on 18 to 20 pieces of paper. (one sentence per sheet). Arrange the sentences on the

Materials

- craft paper
- copy paper
- markers
- sticky notes
- pencils

board so that they snake from the top left to the bottom right.

3 Add decorative elements as you wish—for example, pictures of children at the "Start" square and stars at the "End." (See photo, page 18.)

4 Make pockets on the board to hold sticky notes and pencils. (See page 6 for directions.)

5 Let children unscramble the sentences from start to finish, writing the completed sentences on sticky notes. (They can stick the notes on the sentences to keep track of where they are.) Children can play cooperatively or independently. To keep track of who's played, post a sheet for students to sign when they're finished. Or use sticky notes in a variety of colors to differentiate one group from another.

Variations

° °

Story Scramble: Help children develop a sense of sequence among sentences and of language patterns with this variation. Write sentences from a story on large sticky notes and scramble them on the board. Let children take turns putting the sentences in order to tell the story. Vary the sentences to focus children's attention on different elements, such as words that indicate sequence (first, next, and so on) and beginning/middle/end.

Sequencing Station: Change the board to explore the sequence of events in stories. Write events from a story on separate cards. Place them out of order across the center of the board. Have children sequence the events along the bottom of the board. Children can sign up to change the board every couple of days, replacing the events posted with another series. (Be sure to display the story at the board for reference.)

# Teaching With the Board

For more practice with the sequencing skills children are developing at the board, try these extensions.

Sentence Builders: For additional focus on the sequence of words in a sentence, provide materials for making individual sentence sequence games. Start by writing a sentence on a sentence strip. Cut into individual words, phrases, or both. Let children help you put the sentence back together again. Help them identify clues, such as a period after one word indicating that it is last. Give children sentence strips to make puzzles on their own. Let them trade, trying to put one another's sentences back together.

Scrambled Eggs: Have children write sentences on small strips of paper and cut apart the words in each sentence. Have them write their initials on the back of each word, and then place them in plastic eggs (one sentence per egg). Place eggs in a basket. Children can take the eggs, crack them, and unscramble the sentences.

Dialogue Puzzles: Adapt the board to provide practice with conventions of dialogue. Record things that children say. Write them on pieces of paper (one sentence per piece), scrambling the parts of each sentence. Challenge children to unscramble the sentences to reveal their conversations.

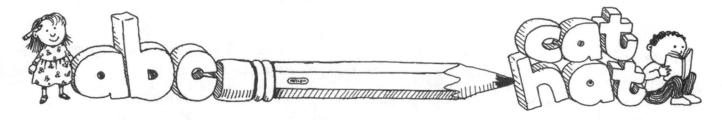

The Sign Board

This high-interest board will have children communicating in sign language, using their hands to spell as well as using pictures of American Sign Language symbols to form words.

BORDER BOX

With a poster showing positions for the manual alphabet and pockets for holding pictures of hands making each letter, you may want to forego a border for this board. In the picture here, some green grass, a cat, and a picture of a child work to pull the display together instead.

LANGUAGE ARTS LINKS

The visual phonics component of this board makes it especially appropriate for use with younger children, though students of all ages will have fun.

TIP

Check teacher supply stores for sign language materials. You can also order a poster of the American Manual Alphabet from the Current Company. Call (800) 848-2848 for more information.

Building the Board

Steps

1. Cover the board with craft paper. Add a heading that says "The Sign Board."

2. Display a poster of the American Manual Alphabet. (See Tip, above.)

Materials

- craft paper
- poster of the American Manual Alphabet
- letter-size envelopes
- pictures of each hand symbol
- stapler
- acetate

3 Staple envelopes to the board. Label with the letters of the alphabet, one per envelope.

4 Enlarge pictures of hand symbols and make several copies. Place pictures in envelopes labeled with the letters they symbolize.

5 Staple a strip of acetate (about 4 by 36 inches) across the bottom of the board to form a pocket.

6 Use the pictures of hand symbols to spell a word or short sentence, placing the symbols in order in the acetate pocket. Can children decode the word(s)?

7 Let children take over, spelling words and messages for classmates to decode and practice spelling in sign language.

8 For a special surprise, welcome children to class each day with a new message in the pocket.

Variations

Words to Know: The American Manual Alphabet is used to spell out names and special words. Other symbols, like the ones pictured here, communicate entire words and phrases. Let children communicate simple expressions in sign, such as *please*, *thank you*, *yes*, and *no*. Meet real-life kids who communicate with sign in *Handtalk School* by Mary Beth Mill and George Ancona (Macmillan, 1991).

Spell It Out: Pin a box to the board and fill it with simple three- or four-letter words written on index cards. When children visit the board, let them select a card and spell it out.

Teaching With the Board

Use sign language as a springboard to science explorations about sound.

Catch That Sound: Our ears help us "catch" sounds. That's why we naturally turn toward sounds we hear—it's easier to hear them. To help children discover the way their ears collect sounds, try this: Have children sit in a circle. Invite a volunteer to sit blindfolded in the middle. Ask children to take turns making soft noises. Challenge the child in the center to find the source of the sound. (The direction alone is sufficient—it may be difficult with a large group to tell exactly who is making the sound.) Encourage children to notice that it's easier to pinpoint where the sound comes from when we face it.

Sound Travels: To demonstrate that sound waves travel—for example, through air—have a volunteer stand at one end of a large space with the remaining children at the other end. Give the volunteer a cap and have him or her shout and drop the cap at the same time. Repeat this several times. What do students notice? (They should see the cap start to fall before they hear the shout. That's because the sound takes a little time to travel to their ears, whereas they can see the cap fall immediately.)

Mirror, Mirror: Hang a mirror near the board. Children love to watch themselves as they sign. This will improve their finger positions too.

The Name Game: Let children take turns finger spelling a classmate's name. Can children guess who it is? For more practice, finger spell children's names throughout the day—for example, as you "call" them to line up.

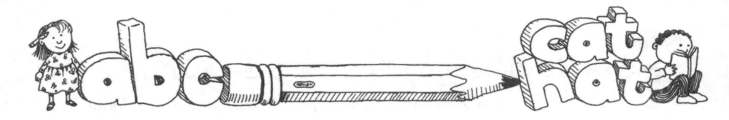

Write On!

Here's how you can create writing spaces that will motivate children to return again and again. Construction paper borders around write-on-wipe-off boards make it easy to customize these writing spaces—letting you change the focus as often as you wish in a matter of minutes! The topics you choose can give children as much or as little direction as you want, letting you meet the varying needs of your students with one display.

BORDER BOX

Frame your white boards with borders that complement the writing topics. Aim for simple but attractive borders that set off students' writing. If you want something that suits a variety of topics, a sparkly frame (wrap cardboard strips with foil and sprinkle with glitter) always adds a special touch.

LANGUAGE ARTS LINKS

These boards invite spontaneous writing. Students can just pick up markers and put down their thoughts—without worrying about spelling, drafts, staying on the lines, or any of the other things that sometimes inhibit writing. As a result, they may express themselves more freely.

# Building the Board

Steps

1 Plan topics for your writing board. For starters, you might want to try the three pictured here: Tell Us About Your Birthday (on their birthdays students can write about birthday wishes, parties, presents, and so on); Special Events (these can be events in students' lives, at school, or in the news); and Create a Story (for freewriting). For more ideas, see Variations, page 26.

Materials

- white boards (26- by 36-inch boards work well, or divide a larger white board)
- dry erase markers
- construction paper
- scissors

TIP

Many newer classrooms have large white boards in place of chalkboards. If yours doesn't, check an office supply or discount store.

2 Hang up the writing boards in an area of your room (or lean them against a board with a chalk ledge), and create simple frames and signs with construction paper. Scalloped edges turn one board into a birthday cake. (Tack up an envelope filled with paper birthday candles that students can add on their special days.)

3 Model and discuss procedures for using the boards (for example, respectful ways to respond to one another's writing).

4 Decide how students will rotate time on the boards (see Tip, below). Then watch their first stories take shape! To save students' writing before the boards are erased, consider keeping a disposable camera on hand (photograph the boards as a set). Display at open school night alongside the boards so that parents can see their children's work.

TIP

To make sure each child gets a turn at the writing boards, you may wish to set up a sign-up sheet each week. Try to maintain some flexibility, however. A child whose dog just had puppies may need to take a turn out of order on the Special Events board to announce the big news! You can also set up board monitors for the week—students who will be in charge of cleaning the boards each day (or week, depending on how often you rotate stories).

Variations

Idea Bank: Stuck for ideas? Here's a bank of ideas to keep your boards in business for a while. Be sure to ask students to share ideas too.

- **Joke Board:** Students write jokes on the board, illustrate them if they choose, then write punch lines upside down.

- **The Daily News:** What's new in students' lives? This is the place to write it down!

- **Poem a Day:** Students can copy favorite poems (including their own) on this board.

- **Math Stories:** Students make up and write down math stories for classmates to solve.

- **Memories:** Let students share mini personal narratives here—favorite memories from the recent past.

- **Pet Tales:** Children can write about their own pets, neighbors' pets, or pets they'd like to have.

- **I Can Do It:** Invite children to share accomplishments here—something they've been working on and achieved.

- **Firsts for Me:** Have children write about firsts in their lives: the first time they rode a bike, stayed over at a friend's house, rode on a roller coaster, lost a tooth, and so on.

- **Conversations:** Invite children to record friendly conversations on the board, using whatever conventions of dialogue they know.

- **Window Watcher:** What do students observe out the window? Encourage them to be creative and specific in their writing—for example, describing a bird and its behavior rather than a more general scene.

- **My Best (Worst) Day:** Give students a chance to share good news (or vent) with this board.

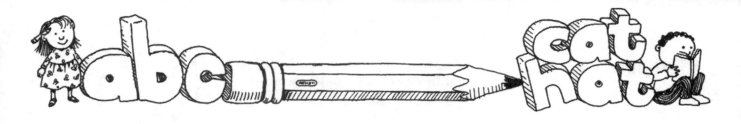

Snip a Book

This display is a must-have. With the directions that follow, you'll prepare a selection of easy-to-make mini-books that children can snip off as they're ready to write new stories. Young authors love the idea of snipping off a little blank book—a great motivator for writing. Be ready for your first batch of these books to be gone in a flash!

BORDER BOX

The display pictured here has a border of scissors and mini-books. Make mini-books by cutting out pictures from book-club flyers, pasting them to slightly larger pieces of folded construction paper, placing blank paper inside, and stapling along the left side.

LANGUAGE ARTS LINK:

This board pulls together key components of any language arts program—writing, publishing, and reading. Even reluctant readers will be motivated by these books—tiny treasures that invite them to read their own words and share them with others. Of course, wordless books are another possibility, allowing children to use only pictures to tell their stories.

Building the Board

Steps

1 Cover a bulletin board with craft paper. Add a title ("Snip a Book") and border.

2 Cut wallpaper, fabric, or paper into strips measuring 49 by 11 inches. If you want the inside cover to match the

Materials

- craft paper
- scissors
- wallpaper, fabric scraps (long pieces), wrapping and other fun papers
- rubber cement
- lined and unlined paper
- paper clips
- sewing machine
- hole punch
- stapler
- scissors
- pushpins
- cardboard or acetate (optional)

TIP

Construction of snip-a-books requires basic sewing (a line down the middle of the stacks of paper). Though each strip of books will only take a minute or two to stitch up, you may want to request parent volunteers to help sew.

outside, cut two lengths and use rubber cement to glue wrong sides together.

3 Cut paper into 10- by 5-inch pieces. Clip each set together at the left and right top corners.

4 Position the first set of pages about a half inch down from the top of the cover material, on the side that will be the inside of the book. Center on either side. Stitch down the middle. Position the second set of pages about an inch below the first, and continue stitching until all sets of pages are sewn to the cover material. (You can vary the number of pages in the books on one strip.)

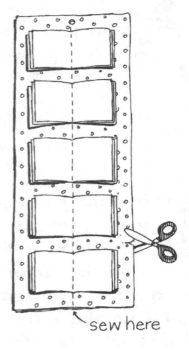

sew here

5 Make additional sets of book strips, varying the width and length of the strips to change the size of the finished books. Allow for space in between each mini-book and at either end.

6 Display books on a bulletin board. Punch a hole in the top center of each and hang from a pin, or staple the top left and right corners.

7 Set up a share space to the side for students' completed mini-books. Frame the space with a simple border to set it off.

8 Make pockets to store scissors. (See page 6.)

9 To snip off their books, have children cut between sets of pages.

Teaching With the Board

Invite children to share their stories with one another by displaying them in the Share space on the board. (Use pushpins to attach them.) There are endless other possibilities for using this board. A couple of suggestions follow:

More Bookmaking Fun:

These mini-books can be just the beginning of students' publishing efforts. Introduce other bookmaking formats periodically to keep interest high. Here are a couple of other quick-and-easy ideas.

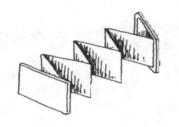

- **Foldout Book:** This version of the Mexican "codex," a foldout picture book used to record events of daily life, is just right for mini-books. To make one, cut two pieces of copy paper in half lengthwise. Tape together to make one long piece. Fold accordion-style to make an eight-page book. Cut two pieces of cardboard 4 1/2 by 5 3/4 inches each. Glue to the first and last pages to make front and back covers.

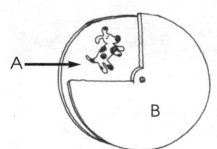

- **Story Wheel:** This circular mini-book has pages that peek out as children turn the wheel. To make one, use a paper plate to trace two circles. Cut them out. Draw two perpendicular lines to divide one circle (A) into four parts or pages. Write a simple story on these pages and illustrate. Cut a window in the second circle (B), as shown, so that one section or page of the other circle will show through. Place B on top of A and use a paper fastener to attach them. Turn the pages of this book by turning the wheel.

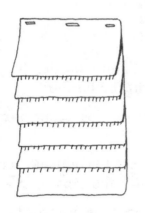

- **Lift-the-Flap Book:** Staple six (or however many pages you want) sheets of paper across the top or side. Starting at the back of the book and moving forward, cut an inch off the bottom of the second to last page. Cut two inches off the bottom of the next page, three off the next page, and so on until all of the pages are staggered as shown. Children can use these books to tell memory stories (use the top page as a cover, and write the numbers 1 through however old they are on the tab of each remaining page, then draw pictures of memories on the inside portion of each page); seasonal stories (make five-page books, use the top page as a cover, write the name of each season on tabs of remaining pages); riddle books (write a riddle on each tab and the answer on the top portion of the page); family books (name of family member on each tab, drawing or description on top portion of the page).

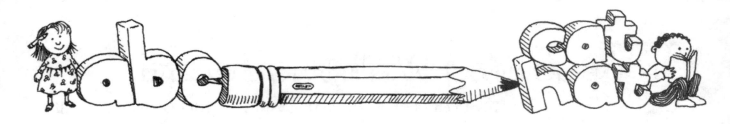

Poetry Place

Bring out the poets in your students with a bulletin board that invites them to play with words every day. Students write worrds and phrases from favorite poems on sentence strips (or magnetic strips if you're using a white board). They can put them together however they like to create poems of their own.

BORDER BOX

Have students cut out and color chunky pencils from butcher paper and write their names on them. Line them up around the edges to create a colorful border.

LANGUAGE ARTS LINKS

When combined with more structured lessons, this board can help you and your students discover the joy in poetry—as they explore families, feelings, and the world around them.

Building the Board

Steps

1 Cover a board with craft paper and add a border. (Or, if you're using a white board, just add the border.)

2 Add a sign that says "Poetry Place" (or any other name your students agree on).

3 Section off several places for students to compose poems. Set aside the rest of the board for word strips.

4 To make the word strips, have students write words or lines from favorite poems on sentence strips. They can write just one word on a strip (and trim it to size) or an

Materials

- butcher paper
- craft paper
- sentence strips
- pushpins
- markers
- collections of poetry (see Classroom Collections)

entire line. (If you're using a white board, you can use magnetic strips for this.)

5 Arrange the strips on the board. Place blank sentence strips in an envelope pinned to the board so that students can easily add to the word strips. Pin up a container of pushpins.

6 Have students combine words on the board to create new poems. (They can use pushpins to hold the word strips in place.) Place a blank book nearby for students to record their finished poems. Soon it will fill up with a class collection of students' poems.

CLASSROOM COLLECTIONS

For a fresh look at poetry, try these collections.

- A *Suitcase of Seaweed and Other Poems* by Janet Wong (McElderry, 1996). The lines in these poems are short, making them manageable for readers of all ages. More important, the poems speak to children of all backgrounds and will inspire them to write about family, school, and other experiences of their own. *Good Luck Gold and Other Poems* (McElderry, 1994) is not to be missed either.

- *Insectlopedia* by Doug Florian (Harcourt Brace, 1998). "They're hip. They hop…They lunge. They plunge…." "The Treehoppers," like the other playful poems in this collection, begs to be read again and again. Other books in the series including *In the Swim*, *On the Wing*, and *Beast Feast* are just as much fun.

- *Popcorn* by James Stevenson (Greenwillow, 1998). These poems are full of feeling and fun, and just the right size for children.

Variations

What Do You Think?

This poetry board invites students' responses to poems they read. Just post a pad of chart paper (making it easy to replace a poem with a new one) and signs that say "About the Poet" and "Tell Us What You Think." Choose a poem to feature, add information about the poet, and post blank paper for responses. (If you're using a white board, as pictured in the photo here, just use a marker to section off the areas on this board.) Students will be happy to take over this board, selecting poems (including their own) to feature and adding information about the poets. Guide their selections to include poems that support your more structured poetry lessons.

Poems in the News: Headlines in the news become first lines for poems with this bulletin board. Begin by having children find and cut out headlines they like. Have them pin the headlines to one section of the bulletin board. Model the activity by writing a poem together, using one of the headlines. Add writing paper and pens to the display and let children compose their own poems. Change the headlines to keep the board fresh. Add completed poems to a class anthology.

Teaching With the Board

You can combine the poetry explorations at the board with mini-lessons to explore poetic devices, such as simile and metaphor, as well as word choice and other elements of writing.

Like What? Introduce simile and metaphor by sharing examples from published poems. (The books listed in Classroom Collections, page 31, are good sources.) Then try an activity suggested by poet Janet Wong. Ask students to compare a family member to an animal, plant, or object. Have them draw pictures first, and then write poems.

Conversation Starters: Rather than use formula poems for children to complete, use published poems to model techniques they can then try themselves. For example, use Janet Wong's "When I Grow Up" (from *A Suitcase of Seaweed*, see page 31) to model conversation poems. ("When I Grow Up" is a conversation between Janet and her grandfather.) Let children begin by recalling conversations they've had (or imagining conversations they'd like to have). Have them write down these conversations. Guide them in making line breaks. As conversations, these poems will be especially rewarding to read aloud.

Words Paint Pictures: Though word choice is important in any kind of writing, it is particularly so in poetry. Share Doug Florian's brief but vivid poems (see Classroom Collections) to explore word choice. Copy one on chart paper and read it aloud, asking children to listen for words that help them picture the subject of the poem. Underline or circle these words and compare them to words the poet might have selected. What makes one word stronger than another?

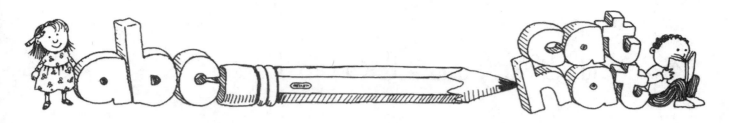

The Daily News

Turn your classroom into a newsroom with a bulletin board that builds speaking, listening, writing, and reading skills in a meaningful context. You can modify the board for any grade, letting students dictate news reports if desired.

BORDER BOX

As pictured here, strips of newspaper make a perfect border. Use spray glue to attach a sheet of newspaper to cardboard, then cut into strips.

LANGUAGE ARTS LINKS:

Students get weekly experience with nonfiction writing and develop their ability to communicate clearly.

TIP

Schedule reporters a month at a time, writing in names on a calendar that you post near the display. Have a backup plan in case of unexpected absences. To include more children each week, or to offer assistance to children who are not ready to report solo, you can assign children to teams.

Building the Board

Steps

1. Cover the board with craft paper. Add a newspaper border and heading (Daily News).

2. Cover construction paper with newspaper, leaving a border all the way around, and add to the display. Attach titles for Headline News, Date, National, and Local, as shown. Use pushpins to attach stacks of chart paper pieces next to both National and Local heads.

3. Tack up a stack of chart paper (you can cut it in halves or quarters) for each day of the week. (You can stick with Monday to Friday or include weekends.) Label.

4. Roll a piece of posterboard so that it resembles a newspaper box. Tape in place. Write "Newspaper" on the outside, and pin it to the bottom right corner of the board.

5. Get ready to tune in to the first report! Assign reporters (see Tip, page 33), then, as a class, discuss the news. (It may help to have the daily paper on hand.) Let the reporter choose news to highlight on each section of the board (local, national, class).

Materials

⊙ craft paper
⊙ newspaper (see Border Box, page 33)
⊙ cardboard
⊙ glue
⊙ construction paper
⊙ scissors
⊙ chart paper
⊙ pushpins
⊙ markers
⊙ posterboard
⊙ tape

Variations

Press Room:

Combine your look at news with other areas of your curriculum—for example, if you're studying space, invite children to look for related stories in the news and add them to a display. Go further by letting children conduct press conferences, each playing the part of a different expert.

◄— Students share news about space from a variety of sources, including newspapers and magazines.

The Daily News:

For young children, try a scaled-down version of the news, inviting one child a day to tell something he or she would like the class to know. Record the child's news on a sheet of chart paper, then let the child illustrate it and hang it up. Together, take a moment to read the news again a little later. Then roll it up to share at home.

Teaching With the Board

This board will not only model nonfiction writing but will help create a newsroom-like atmosphere in your classroom—where students feel at home discussing and writing about the news near and far. Following are three ways to do more with the board:

A Week at a Glance: Bind news reports for each week into a book. Add front and back covers, staple along the top or left side, and date. Let each week's reporters take turns sharing the news at home.

Sloppy Copy: What can you do about writer's block in your classroom? In *Free to Write* (Heinemann, 1995), journalist Roy Peter Clark suggests having them write on deadline like journalists. "Have students write like the dickens for five or ten minutes without stopping. The result is 'sloppy copy,' of course, but students are astonished at how quickly they fill up a page." You may be too! Students can rewrite these quick pieces, looking for details they want to spend more time developing.

All the News: Let students take their reporting skills further by publishing a newsletter to send home on a regular basis. (You might start with once a month.) There are many ways to involve students—in writing stories, doing artwork, editing, arranging stories and art on paper for printing, and so on. Think about including regular "departments," such as upcoming events and write-ups of recent special activities.

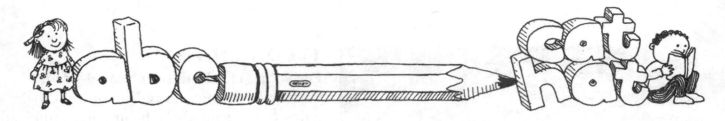

Take a Memo!

Think of all the memos you get. There's lots of reading in those little pieces of paper! Memos can also offer students plenty of meaningful reasons to read. The giant memo board here lets you and your students make them big enough for everyone to read. You can vary the memo topics to connect language arts with any subject.

BORDER BOX

Brainstorm reasons to write memos—for example, to make announcements, to offer reminders, and to let people know they did a good job. List the ideas on sentence strips and use them to make a border.

LANGUAGE ARTS LINK

Like memos in the workplace, these memos give children real-life reasons to write and read. You can also use memos to build a bridge to nonfiction writing. (See Teaching With the Board, page 37.)

TIP

Though the memo board shown here is set up on a bulletin board, a wall space will do just as well. Make sure you locate the chart-size setup where it will be easily visible to children.

Building the Board

Steps

1 Cover a wall space with craft paper. Add a heading that says "The Memo Board."

2 Paint a piece of cardboard brown. Cut silver paper to look like a clip. Glue the clip to the top of the cardboard to make a clipboard. Tack chart paper to the clipboard.

Materials

- craft paper
- cardboard
- brown paint, paintbrush
- silver paper
- scissors
- glue
- pushpins
- chart paper
- small box, manila envelope
- standard-size clipboard
- writing paper, markers

3 Open up one side of the box and attach to the wall near the clipboard. Write "Responses" on the box. Cut a small manila envelope in half, fill with small slips of paper, and attach next to the small box.

4 Place a real clipboard with paper to one side so that children can write mini-memos for classmates.

5 Write the first memo to model the format for students. Add lines for To, From, Date, and Subject to make it look like the real thing! Invite children to add to the memo board when they have information to share. Children can respond to memos on slips of paper and place them in the box.

Teaching With the Board

Memos can be the start of a nonfiction spree in your classroom. Try these ideas to encourage children's interest in and awareness of this genre.

Reasons for Writing: Memos are a fun way to weave informational writing into the school day. Start by sharing some of the memos you get. These might be notices about policies, upcoming workshops, vacation schedules, and so on. Let children study the memos to discover what they all have in common. Talk about abbreviations (*memo* is short for "memorandum," *re* for "regarding"). Notice that memos include this basic information: who the memo is to, who it is from, what the date is, and what the memo is about. Let children tell how each piece of information helps the reader. Follow up by looking at language and length. Notice that memos are usually short—and therefore the writer needs to use concise language. Make copies of the memo form on page 38 for children to use on their own. (Store them at the writing center or in an envelope on the board.)

Just for You: Use memos to give individual messages to children. For example, if a child's parent calls to say that he or she will be picking up the child early, put the information in a memo for the child. Children can use the same technique to share important information with you. (This is a great way for them to tell you about problems they're having too—for example, on the playground.)

Memo

To: _____

From: _____

Date: _____

Re: _____

_____

_____

_____

Memo

To: _____

From: _____

Date: _____

Re: _____

_____

_____

_____

38

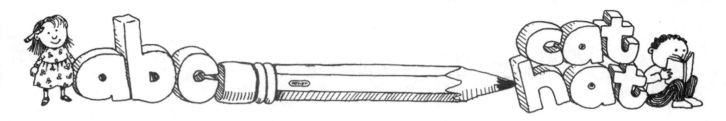

Chitchat Board

Children put themselves in the places of characters pictured on the board and then write the conversations that might take place between them.

BORDER BOX
Let children draw pictures of their faces and then connect speech balloons. When they've got something to add to the conversation on the board, they can fill in their speech balloons, replacing them as needed to get in on new conversations.

LANGUAGE ARTS LINK

A fun board for any age, this one helps children learn conventions of conversations—starting with the idea that they go two ways. Having children write down conversations, even imaginary ones, also strengthens the link between oral and written language. Encouraging children to record their conversations in complete sentences will further strengthen both speaking and writing skills and help them learn to communicate more complete thoughts.

 **Building the Board**

Steps

1 Cover the bulletin board with craft paper and add a sign that reads "The Chitchat Board."

2 Add a border, if desired. (See Border Box, page 39.)

3 Pin up pictures of two characters. (See Conversation Starters, page 41, for suggestions.)

4 Make speech balloons from newsprint, cutting out stacks from each color. Tack up one next to each character. Store extras on the board in a two-pocket folder.

5 Tack up a box of markers. Let children decide what the characters are saying and write the conversations in the speech balloons.

6 Invite two students to record a conversation. As with a real conversation, one will need to start, the other will follow. Encouraging them to use complete sentences rather than the fragments we sometimes hear in conversation will enable children to communicate more effectively.

7 When one conversation is complete and another pair of students is ready to create their own dialogue, just have them replace the speech balloons with fresh newsprint. Save completed conversations for follow-up activities. (See Teaching With the Board, page 41.)

Materials

- ⊙ craft paper
- ⊙ newsprint (two colors)
- ⊙ scissors
- ⊙ pushpins
- ⊙ pocket folder
- ⊙ markers
- ⊙ cardboard and clear contact paper (optional)

TIP

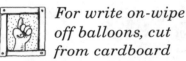 *For write on-wipe off balloons, cut from cardboard and laminate. Supply white board markers or overhead pens for writing.*

Variation

Picture Talk: Have children cut out pictures of people from magazines and mount two or more on tagboard or construction paper. Tack a pocket folder to the board to hold materials. Place pictures on one side, blank speech bubbles on the other. Children can select pictures, paste on speech bubbles, and write conversations.

Teaching With the Board

Draw on children's lives—books they read, people they know, comics they like—to teach with this board. Suggestions follow.

Conversation Starters:

Pictured is a conversation between a boy and a woman who children have decided is the boy's mother. They've also supplied the conversation—the boy is lost. His mother reassures him and promises to be "rite there." In preparation for your chitchat board, create several sets of conversation-starter characters.

(This is a good way to tie in characters from literature.) Then let children take over, creating and sharing their own. Suggestions for starter sets follow:

- the Wolf and Grandma (from Little Red Riding Hood)
- Jack and the Giant (from Jack and the Beanstalk)
- a lion and a mouse
- characters from favorite children's books
- a child and the President
- a child and a sports figure

Comic Strip Stories:

A favorite of many children, comic strips are great tools for teaching conversation "rules"—and conventions of dialogue in writing. Mount comic strips on cardboard and cut apart. Use as a sequencing task. (Store in resealable bags.)

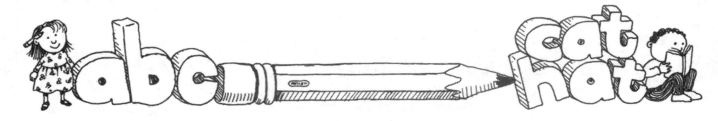

The Friendship Message Center

Students make paper dolls of themselves, then use sticky notes to give messages to one another. Whether children are writing messages to classmates to exchange important information about a class project or dashing off a note to say, "I like your hat," this board will give students reasons to write every day.

BORDER BOX

For a fun, easy border, have children make and decorate strings of paper dolls (about six inches high). Connect each child's cutouts to frame the board. (See page 7 for directions.)

LANGUAGE ARTS LINKS

Writing and reading messages are literacy skills that students will use again and again in real life.

TIP

For write on-wipe off balloons, cut from cardboard and laminate. Supply white board markers or overhead pens for writing. Monitor the board to make sure all students get messages from time to time. Model appropriate messages to post. Ask students to tell you how they will know if a message they want to post is appropriate. (For example, they can ask themselves, "Will this message hurt anyone's feelings?" If the answer is no, the message is okay.)

Building the Board

Steps

1. Cover the background as desired. Add a sign that says "Friendship Message Center."

2. Have children create large paper dolls of themselves. Let them add yarn hair, wallpaper clothes, and other details to decorate. Arrange dolls on the board.

3. Demonstrate how to leave someone a message by writing a note to a student and sticking it on his or her paper doll. As you write the message, let students suggest important information to include, such as your name. Discuss other important details a message might contain, such as who the message is from, the date and time it was left, and so on.

4. Staple a couple of small boxes (open at the top) to the board to hold sticky-note pads and pencils. Your message center is open for business!

Materials

- craft paper (the board uses blue and green)
- construction paper
- scissors
- yarn, wallpaper scraps, and other supplies for decorating paper dolls
- pushpins
- sticky notes
- pencils
- 2 small boxes

Variations

Question of the Week: Prepare a set of questions for the board ahead of time, then tack up a new one each week. Have students respond by writing their answers on sticky notes and posting them on their paper doll figures. Use the information students gather for graphing activities and to discover more about ways in which students are alike and different. (They can use the sticky notes to make the graph after they respond to the questions.)

- How old are you?
- What is your favorite food (place to go, book, color, and so on)?
- How many people are in your family?
- When is your birthday?

TIP

Encourage children to respond in complete sentences to develop their ability to expand on ideas.

⊙ What is your favorite season?

⊙ What is your favorite time of day?

⊙ What time do you go to bed?

Friends Share Books: Have children create mini-books, poems, or pictures to tack to their paper dolls. Students can borrow the materials, returning them to their spots when done.

A Change of Clothes: Provide tagboard patterns to make clothes, along with wallpaper, construction paper, and so on. Let children change their paper doll's clothes as they wish.

Teaching With the Board

Students may already be familiar with taking messages at home. Reinforce this important skill with this activity.

Take a Message: Stock a dramatic-play center with old or toy telephones and let children practice giving and taking messages. Introduce the activity by inviting children who take phone messages at home to show how it's done. Encourage children to notice that there is more than one way to answer a phone. Discuss the kinds of information that message recipients appreciate having, such as name, date, time, and nature of call. Then let children pair up to try it themselves.

What's Missing? Reinforce the importance of giving complete messages with this activity. Write messages on index cards, leaving a piece of information out of each one—for example, "Be there at 8:30." Let children pick cards from the box, tell what information is missing, then rewrite the messages to make them complete.

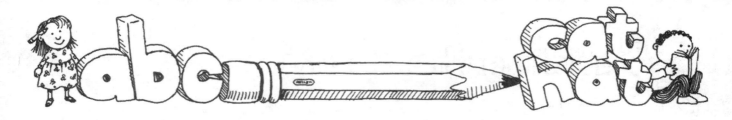

What I Like About You

This bulletin board makes everyone feel special—and shows the powerful effect kind words can have (on both the giving and receiving end). It's easy to maintain and will promote a spirit of cooperation and goodwill in your classroom that can only be a boost to learning. For each student featured on the board, students will create pages full of positive comments. When you take these down to set up for a new student, you can bind them into a book for the child to proudly share at home.

BORDER BOX

Let students use colorful markers and sentence strips to write words that could describe someone special—for example, *extraordinary, kind, caring, fair, friendly,* and so on. Glue them to strips of paper to make a border.

LANGUAGE ARTS LINK

Students express what they like about others in words, exploring synonymns and specific language at the same time.

TIP

The basic elements of this board—chart paper and markers—don't change. Just set up the display, then every week or two when you're ready to spotlight a new student, change the photos, pictures, and other items that celebrate that child.

 # Building the Board

Steps

Materials

- craft paper
- markers
- sentence strips
- pushpins
- chart paper
- hole punch
- photos of children
- name tags
- glue

TIP

 Although photos are not essential to this board, they do add a nice touch. You might prepare ahead for this by requesting that parents send in photos of their children. Or use a Polaroid camera to take pictures of children as their turns come up at the board.

1 Cover a display space with craft paper and create a heading that says "Special Person." Let students prepare the border. (See Border Box, page 45.)

2 Tack up a stack of chart paper to the board. Write the words "Tell us what you like about _____" on a sentence strip and display above the chart paper.

3 Have each child write his or her name on a sentence strip, decorate if desired, and trim. Punch a hole in each card. Use a pushpin to hang name tags above the sentence.

4 Make the first student selection a surprise, setting up the board when students are out of the room. Pin the child's name in place to complete the sentence, and display photos and a colorful name tag as shown in the photo on page 45.

5 Let children take care of the rest, drawing and displaying pictures for the special person, writing comments on the chart, and so on.

6 When you're ready to switch students, have a couple of volunteers glue pictures to chart paper and make a cover. Put the cover page together with the picture and comment pages to make a book for the child to keep.

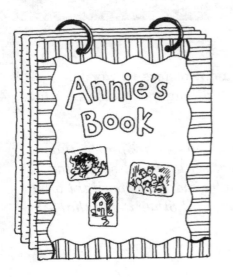

Annie's Book

Teaching With the Board

Use this bulletin board to create momentum in your classroom for the following related activities.

Special Stories: To model essay-writing, begin by using comments children recorded about a classmate, showing how the reasons or facts they give support the statement that the child is special. Together, rewrite the comments to tell a cohesive story about the child. Follow up by letting children write essays about special people in their lives. Framed by colorful construction paper borders, these stories make special gifts.

Home-School Connection: Invite parents to celebrate the ways their children are special too. For each child featured, ask the parents or another special adult in the child's life to send in a note about the child and what makes him or her special. Add the note to the board, and watch that child beam!

Special Storybook Characters: Use children's literature to explore qualities of favorite characters. What makes them special? For example, in *Sheila Rae the Brave* by Kevin Henkes (Greenwillow, 1987), students might appreciate Sheila Rae's outgoing nature and her sister Louise's more quiet strengths. Create character webs to show what is special about characters in books you read.

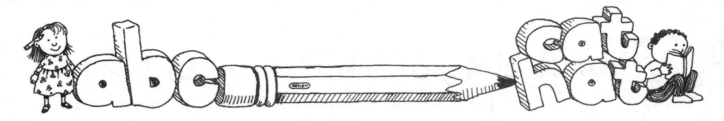

Story Boards

There's something about long strips on a board that is conducive to writing. Students enjoy visiting this board to add on to stories already started. These can be fiction or nonfiction and can change with the season or topic. Students enjoy coming up with their own ideas for creating stories on this board too.

BORDER BOX

The photo here pictures a borderless board. If you'd like to add a border to yours, try writing a collaborative story on adding machine tape that goes all the way around your board. For a seasonal border, create a repeating pattern—for example, flowers in spring.

LANGUAGE ARTS LINK

Students come up with story ideas, then collaborate to tell stories from beginning to end. In the process, they learn about sequencing, sentence structure, and story structure. You can guide the story topics to develop creative writing skills or to strengthen nonfiction writing.

# Building the Board

Steps

Materials

- craft or mural paper
- paint, paintbrushes
- construction paper
- scissors
- stapler
- pushpins
- sentence strips
- markers

TIP

 To ensure that all students have a chance to add to this board, let them draw numbers and take turns in order.

1 Enlist students' help in creating a background for this board. A seasonal board may come in handy, allowing you leave it up for an extended period of time. A topic-related board will work too, giving children a place to connect language arts with learning activities across the curriculum. The background in the display shown on page 48 pictures a spring scene, perfect for sunny-day stories. Students can also add to the display scene as their stories progress.

2 Add long, narrow strips of paper to the board, cut with a slight wave. Staple or pin strips to the board to create lines for writing.

3 Invite a child to start a story. The story may be fiction or nonfiction. Other children can take turns adding on to tell the middle and end. (See Teaching With the Board for tips on teaching about beginnings, middles, and endings.)

4 When a story is complete and students want to start a new one, remove and stack the strips. Then tack them vertically on the board and label. Children can take them down as they wish to read the stories, sequence them, and so on.

Variations

Pick a Strip: Number sentence strips starting with one. Punch a hole at the end of each and hang on the board from a straight pin. (Children will be able to take strips off the board one at a time without taking them all down.) Let one child begin by taking strip 1, posting it on the board, and starting a story. Another child can take strip 2 and add to the story. This continues until one child decides to wrap up the story.

Behind the Bush: Students in one class came up with their own variation, hiding parts of the story behind big bushes they added to the display.

Rebus Stories: Children will have fun drawing pictures and substituting them for some of the words in their stories.

Teaching With the Board

The Story Board is a good opportunity for a mini-lesson or two on beginnings, middles, and endings of stories.

Story Structure: As you share children's books with students, discuss beginnings, middles, and endings. What makes a beginning effective and an ending satisfying? Help children identify details and events that keep the middle of a story moving. To draw students' attention to the beginnings, middles, and endings of stories they build on the board, label the first few strips "beginning," the next three or four "middle," and the last couple "ending." This general structure will help them think about the section of the story they're writing and how best to start or add to a story.

All in a Day: What went on in the last 24 hours of your students' lives? Post a class journal to record details of the day. Invite students to look for story starters in those details. Use the ideas to start new stories on the board. Be sure to have children take turns choosing the story starters for the board so that everyone has a chance.

Experimenting With Endings: As you share stories with memorable endings, stop near the end and ask children to suggest possible endings. Try each of them out, rereading the last couple of pages and inserting the various endings. Then share the author's ending. Is it like any of those suggested by your students? Keep a class learning log of endings. Have children record titles and what they like about the endings.

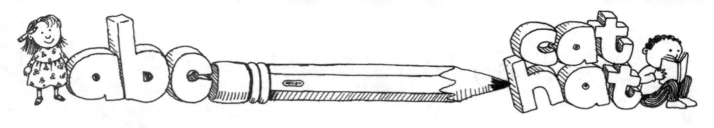

Camouflage Capers

Children make and hide butterflies around the classroom in plain sight, camouflaging them against objects. When students spot butterflies, they add them to the board with caption cards describing exactly where they found them. This board can go on as long as student interest lasts (for hide-and-seek games like this, that can be some time). It makes a handy spring or fall (change the background) science connection and gives observation skills a good workout, all while boosting descriptive writing skills.

LANGUAGE ARTS LINKS

As children describe where they found the butterflies, they'll strengthen their writing skills, especially their ability to choose specific words. Children also like to read this board, making it an inviting print resource for your room.

TIP

Some butterflies will be so well hidden that they'll keep turning up—long after you've changed the board. If this happens, set aside a corner of the blackboard or a sheet of chart paper on a wall where students can continue to display butterflies and their descriptions.

BORDER BOX

Provide assorted papers and experiment with torn paper and collage to create a border of colorful butterflies for this board.

# Building the Board

Steps

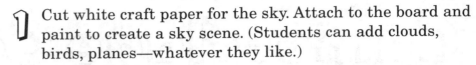

1 Cut white craft paper for the sky. Attach to the board and paint to create a sky scene. (Students can add clouds, birds, planes—whatever they like.)

Materials

- craft paper (white and green)
- scissors
- paint, paintbrushes
- stapler or pushpins
- butterfly template (see page 54)

2 Cut green paper in the shapes of hills. Overlap on the board and pin in place. Use paint to add tiny flowers, trees, and other details.

3 Let students design the title (Camouflage Capers) and write definitions for each word. Place them at the top of the display.

4 Invite students to design butterflies that will be camouflaged by something in the room. In the close-up here, you can see that one student created a polka-dot wing design to blend in with the dress of a papier-mâché person. Children can draw their own butterflies or use the template on page 54 as a pattern.

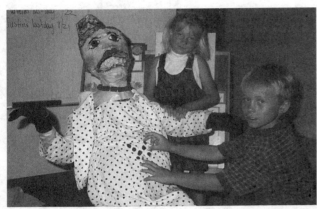

5 Arrange to have children hide their butterflies. When children spot butterflies, have them write captions that explain where they were and how they were camouflaged. Have children arrange both butterflies and captions on the board.

6 Encourage children to contribute to the display as they like, adding butterfly poems, stories, even plants that a butterfly might eat. Watch the display grow!

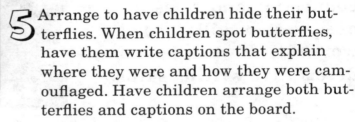# Teaching With the Board

From learning to write clear directions to exploring camouflage and symmetry, this bulletin board has varied learning connections.

Writing Mini-Lesson: As children write captions telling where they found their butterflies, they'll get practice writing clear explanations, a useful life skill. Bring small groups of children together to reread some of their captions. Which words help make the directions clear? (For a related board, see Tell Me How, page 70.)

The Science of Camouflage: Link the language arts in this display with a science focus on camouflage. Take a close-up look at a butterfly (or look at pictures). Ask: "How do you think a butterfly's colors, patterns, and shape help it survive in nature?" Guide children to understand that camouflage is like a disguise. Animals that are camouflaged, such as a walking stick that looks like the branch it sits on, can escape predators by blending into their surroundings.

Play a quick game to reinforce the concept of camouflage. Cut yarn in browns, greens, yellows, reds, and blues into four-inch pieces. (Cut an equal number of each color.) Mark off a large space in a grassy area and, while children's eyes are closed, sprinkle the yarn around the area. (Count the number of pieces first.) Have children uncover their eyes and then give them one minute to find as many pieces as they can. Sort by color. Which color did students find most of? Fewest? What explanation can they give? (The grassy-colored pieces of yarn are camouflaged and harder to spot.) For more information, share *How to Hide an Octopus and Other Sea Creatures* by Ruth Heller (Putnam, 1992) and *We Hide, You Seek* by Jose Aruego (Morrow, 1983).

Symmetry in Nature: Science, math, and art come into play with the concept of symmetry, which children can observe in a butterfly's wing design as well as its wing and leg structure. Ask: "Where else in nature do we see symmetry?" (For example, in other insects,

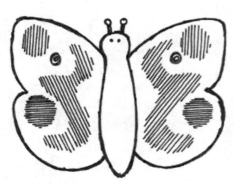

in maple tree seeds, in the way leaves grow on stems.) Demonstrate the concept of symmetry with this simple activity. Make a copy of the butterfly template (see page 54) for each child. Ask children to paint a design on one wing and then fold the paper in half. Have them press lightly and then open their butterflies. Ask children to describe what they see. (The wings will have symmetrical designs.) Encourage children to be aware of symmetry as they draw designs on the butterflies they camouflage in the classroom.

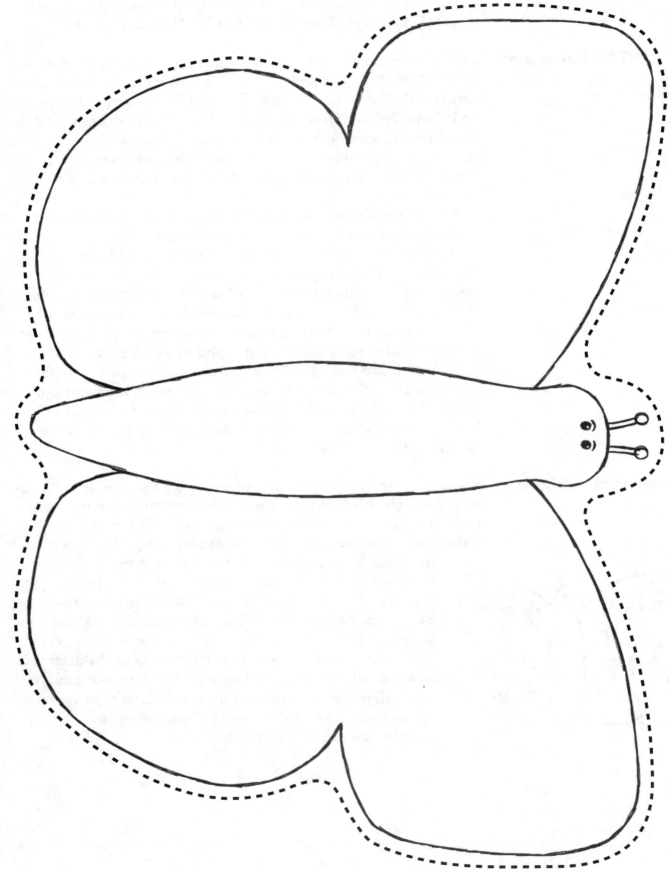

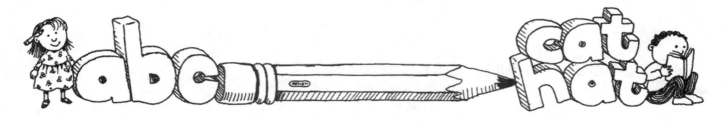

Unfold a Story

Students unfold these stories a page at a time, adding on to build books. The photo here shows three books on one board, but you can unfold a single story anywhere you have a long narrow space available. Try placing several in different spots around the room. The hallway outside your classroom is another good location—and it will keep passersby coming back to read each new page.

LANGUAGE ARTS LINK

Depending on the story topic (see Variations, page 56), these stories can be designed to encourage children to think about beginnings, middles, and endings. Whether they're writing fiction or nonfiction, they'll need to read the pages leading up to the new page and build logical connections to what's already been written.

BORDER BOX

The board pictured here has a simple frame of stars. For another cute border, fold strips of colored craft paper (about 2 1/2 inches wide) accordion-style.

Scholastic Professional Books, 1998

Building the Board

Steps

Materials
- craft paper (colored and white)
- scissors
- markers
- pushpins

1 Cover the bulletin board with craft paper and add a heading that says "Watch the Stories Unfold."

2 Cut white craft paper into 80- by 10-inch strips.

3 Draw lines every 10 inches on the strip to create seven 10-inch-wide pages and a cover. Starting at the right, fold one page over the next, as shown. Do not fold over the last page—this will serve as a cover.

4 Write the title of the book on the cover, then use push-pins to tack the book to the left side of the board.

5 To write in the book, students can remove the tacks and unfold to reveal one page at a time (then tack pages in place again). Students can continue in this way to reveal and write on each additional page.

TIP

 To give all students a chance to interact with what is sure to be a popular board, post a sign-up sheet for adding on to stories. Keep in mind that while students may each fill up a page, there's no need to require this. Children may add on a sentence or two or more, then let another child take over.

Variations

The Facts Unfold: On each new page, students write down subject, name, and related facts. Set up several of these Unfold-a-Story boards during science and social studies units to encourage children to share information on different subjects they're studying.

An Unusual Event Unfolds: Brainstorm unusual events (real or make-believe) and use them to start off stories. Children will be proud to see their ideas up on the board and excited to see how their ideas evolve into stories.

A Fairy Tale Unfolds: Let children suggest favorite fairy tales to retell. To get their creative juices flowing, share some unusual retellings of fairy tales or folktales. For example:

The True Story of the Three Little Pigs by Jon Scieszka (Viking, 1989). The wolf tells his side of the story.

Yeh-Shen: A Cinderella Story From China by Ed Young (Philomel, 1982). This version features a magic fish instead of a fairy godmother.

A Poem Unfolds: Start a collaborative poem. Let children build on the poem from one page to the next. Remind students that a poem can be like a tiny story—and that lines do not have to rhyme.

Teaching With the Board

Explore beginnings, middles, and endings with these ideas.

Blockbuster Beginnings: Children who start an unfold-a-story book will want to pay special attention to leads. Plan a mini-lesson to look at ways authors start stories and make readers want to continue. Techniques to consider include:

- asking a question.
- using a quote.
- sharing an interesting fact.
- setting the scene.
- introducing characters' personalities.
- using suspense.

Pull together examples from children's literature and/or newspaper articles that feature strong leads. Read them aloud and ask students to describe the beginnings. Identify the type of lead each author used. Follow up by suggesting a topic or two. Let children try writing different kinds of leads for the topic. Invite students to discuss leads they think work best as well as those they weren't satisfied with.

Details, Details: Help children develop the middle sections of their stories with a mini-lesson on adding details. This one, adapted from *25 Mini-Lessons for Teaching Writing* by Adele Fiderer (Scholastic Professional Books, 1997), is quick, easy, and fun. Start by choosing a sentence to develop—for example, "The storm was awesome." Have students take turns supplying details to show how spooky the night was—for example, "The wind howled all night." Follow up by selecting sentences from students' own writing and discussing possible details to add.

By the time students are done, they'll have added more than enough details to give readers a good picture of the stormy night—and gotten a good idea of how they can add descriptive details to their own stories, including the unfold-a-story books.

Effective Endings:

Sooner or later, the unfold-a-story books will come to an end. Share examples of effective endings from children's literature to model various techniques. Suggestions follow:

Math Curse by Jon Scieszka (Viking, 1995). The ending of this book lets readers know that the story is definitely not over. "I've broken the math curse. I can solve any problem and life is just great until science class, when Mr. Newton says, "You know, you can think of almost everything as a science experiment..."

Officer Buckle and Gloria by Peggy Rathman (Putnam, 1995). A police officer who shares safety tips at schools is upstaged by his more animated police dog. His feelings get hurt, but the two kiss and make up at the end and readers get one last tip: "Always stick with your buddy." Ask: "What clues does the author give you that lead up to this ending? How does this ending pull the story together?"

The Empty Pot by Demi (Henry Holt, 1990). In this story of courage and integrity, an emperor sets out to choose a successor to the throne. He gives all the children special flower seeds and tells them to return in a year. Whoever grows the best flowers will succeed him to the throne. In a surprise ending, the one child who returns with an empty pot, unable to get his seed to grow, is made emperor.

All the Places to Love by Patricia MacLachlan (HarperCollins, 1994). When Eli is born, his grandmother holds him up to an open window so that the first thing he sees is "all the places to love." At the story's end, Eli's got a new sister—and he's thinking about the day when he can show *her* all the places to love.

The Relatives Came by Cynthia Rylant (Bradbury, 1985). This rollicking story starts with a family leaving Virginia to visit relatives up north. It ends with them driving home, looking ahead to next year and another visit with the relatives.

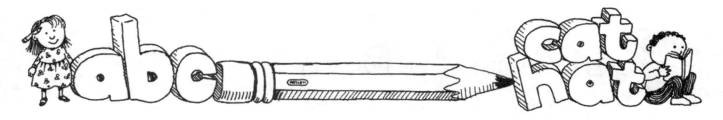

Fairy Tale Mail

You supply the chart paper for a board that connects reading and writing—your students will keep it going by suggesting fairy tale characters to write to. A "Coming Up Next" feature keeps student interest strong.

LANGUAGE ARTS LINKS

Students practice friendly letter-writing on a board that invites them to explore character development. Stocking a nearby basket with copies of fairy tales encourages further exploration of this genre. Letters tucked in envelopes around the border invite more reading and writing.

BORDER BOX

The border pictured here is made by tacking up envelopes around the perimeter. Write a few letters to fairy tale characters and place them in the envelopes. Students can check the envelopes at the board to discover these little treasures. They'll be inspired to add their own too!

Building the Board

Steps

1 Cover the bulletin board with craft paper. Add a heading that reads "Fairy Tale Mail" and a smaller heading that reads "Coming Up Next…"

2 Create a border by stapling envelopes addressed to various fairy tale characters around the outside edges. Leave some blank for students to address.

3 Fold a large sheet of construction paper to make a pocket. Write "Paper Holder" on it and staple it to the board. Roll chart paper and place it in the pocket. (See page 6.)

4 Tack up four sheets of chart paper to get children started. Attach a picture of a fairy tale character to each. Write one letter yourself if students need a model.

5 Let children write letters (large and small), read letters, and add pictures of new fairy tale characters to the "Coming Up Next…" spot.

Materials

⊙ craft paper
⊙ stapler
⊙ letter-size envelopes
⊙ construction paper
⊙ chart paper
⊙ pushpins
⊙ markers

Letter Starters

Though children will surely come up with their own ideas for fairy tale letters, you may at times want to direct their attention to specific things, such as a character's qualities, motivation for doing something, or feelings about an event. Children can consider the following questions as they write to their fairy tale friends:

Character Development:
⊙ What qualities does this character possess that you admire?

Setting:
⊙ How do you picture the place where the story happens? What do you like about it? What would you tell the character about the place where you live?

Conflict:
⊙ What do you think of the way the character solved the problem? Have you ever had a similar problem? What are some other ways of solving a problem like this?

INTERACTIVE BULLETIN BOARDS • LANGUAGE ARTS
Scholastic Professional Books, 1998

Variations

Make a Mini-Play: Display a fairy tale or book character on the board. Have one child ask the character a question and another answer as that character. Let children read the dialogue aloud as a mini-play.

What Would You Do? Display a series of fairy tale or book characters who present clear problems. Have children write letters to the characters telling what they would have done in their place. (For example, Cinderella leaves the ball to meet her twelve o'clock deadline. Would children have done the same thing?)

Teaching With the Board

Use the following ideas to help children discover the satisfaction and pleasure letter-writing can bring.

Keep in Touch: Letter-writing can be a source of great pleasure for students. Trading notes with friends can grow to include writing newsy letters to parents, pen pals, and more. Introduce the parts of a friendly letter by sharing real letters. Together, look for the heading (sender's address), salutation (greeting), body (the writer's thoughts), closing, and signature. Brainstorm ideas for friendly letters. For example, they can:

⊙ tell about a trip.

⊙ describe something that happened at home or school.

⊙ share thoughts and feelings.

⊙ tell about an activity, such as soccer or a book club.

Building on Books: Substitute favorite children's book characters for fairy tale characters on the board. Have children suggest book characters they'd like to write to and then work in teams to make pictures of them to display on the board. Rotate characters at the display to include all of children's suggestions. Leave the letter-writing wide open, or suggest a direction—for example, children might write Arthur (of the Marc Brown series) about something they have in common, George and Martha about friendship problems, and Frog and Toad about their own adventures. Children can take their letter-writing further and write the authors or illustrators of favorite books. (In most cases, you can send these letters to the publisher.)

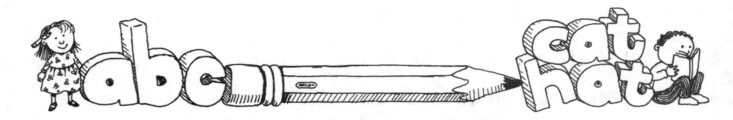

Bag a Story

Paper bags on a board are filled with pictures that represent character, setting, and conflict. Students select one or more of each at random to build stories!

BORDER BOX

Overlap small brown paper sacks around the board or open them for a 3-D border. For a colorful border, tack up pictures that represent character, conflict, and setting to strips of brown paper. Children can use these pictures in addition to the ones in the bags to put their stories together.

LANGUAGE ARTS LINKS

As students invent connections that tie their character, setting, and conflict pictures together, they'll develop their ability to weave key elements of a story into a cohesive whole. In subsequent writing unaided by picture prompts, watch for growth in students' attention to logical connections and detail.

Building the Board

Steps

Materials

- butcher paper (or large brown bags)
- paper lunch bags
- pictures (drawn or cut from magazines)
- construction paper

1 Cover a board with brown paper. Add a heading that says "Bag a Story."

2 Fold the tops of three lunch bags down a few times. Label one "character," another "setting," and the third "problem/conflict." Staple the back of each bag to the board.

3 Fill the character and setting bags with representative pictures. Fill the third bag with descriptions of problems or conflicts. To get your Bag-a-Story board going, we've supplied a few conflict cards. (See Bag a Story: Problem/Conflict Cards, page 65.)

4 Make a pocket to hold extra paper bags by folding up the bottom third of large sheet of construction paper and stapling along the sides. Staple or tack to the board and stock with bags.

5 Let children visit the board, each taking an empty bag and filling it with at least one picture from each bag.

6 Have children use the pictures and problem/conflict cards to tell stories, returning bags and story elements to the board when they're finished. Encourage them to pay close attention to detail in both character and setting pictures. Ask: "What do the details tell you about the characters/places?"

7 Freshen your story bags periodically by adding new pictures and descriptions. Invite students to help out, adding their own pictures and descriptions to the bags.

Teaching With the Board

Take a close-up look at character, setting, and conflict with these mini-lessons.

Character Webs: Share a story that has a memorable character. *Your Move* by Eve Bunting (Harcourt Brace, 1998) and *The Balancing Girl* by Bernice Rabe (Dutton, 1981) are two possibilities. After reading, ask: "What words describe the character(s) in this book?" Record students' ideas on a character web.

Senses and Settings Go Together: Help children see how they can use their senses to add details to their settings. Begin by sharing a passage from a story that is rich with sensory images. The following sentence from *Charlotte's Web* by E. B. White (HarperCollins, 1952) is just right: "All morning you could hear the rattle of the machine as it went round and round, while the tall grass fell down behind the cutter bar in long green swatches." Write the words *sound*, *taste*, *smell*, *sight*, and *touch* on chart paper. Ask children to describe how the passage helps them picture the setting. Can they hear the machine rattling? See the tall grass fall? Smell the freshly cut grass?

Conflict: Explore the kinds of conflicts that make good stories by taking a look at problems in children's own lives. Ask: "How does the weather sometimes cause problems for you?" (Bad weather might prevent a child from playing at a friend's house.) "What are some of the conflicts you sometimes have with friends or family members?" (Two friends might disagree over who gets to keep a dime that they both saw on the sidewalk at the same time.) "What kinds of conflicts do you sometimes have with yourself?" (A child may see another child being teased and want to help but be worried that he or she will be teased as a result.) Follow up by sharing children's literature that represents each of these basic kinds of conflict. For example:

- *Brave Irene* by William Steig (Farrar, Straus & Giroux, 1986). A young girl battles a snowstorm to deliver the gown her sick mother has sewn for the duchess.

- *Stevie* by John Steptoe (HarperCollins, 1969). A young boy dislikes looking after his younger foster brother—then misses him when he's gone.

- *Spinky Sulks* by William Steig (Farrar, Straus & Giroux, 1988). A boy goes into a big sulk, then has to find a way to save face getting out of it.

A character in the story has a problem with one or more of the other characters.

You have been asked by a friend to keep a secret. You don't know what to do.

You (or other characters) are playing outside. The weather changes suddenly.

You (or other characters) have been magically transported to someplace you've never been. What happens there? How will you get back?

Things are turning up missing in the place where your story is set. You're the only one who notices.

Aliens have just landed in the place where your story is set.

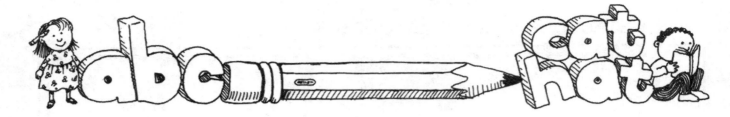
The List Board

This board can change as quickly as you can put up a fresh sheet of chart paper. Use it to enrich both reading and writing in an almost endless number of ways—across your curriculum.

BORDER BOX

The board pictured here has a border made of—what else?—lists! Invite students to make their own "Grocery" and "To Do" lists for the border or suggest their own ideas, such as birthday lists.

LANGUAGE ARTS LINKS

From inviting children to list words that can take the place of "said," to featuring new vocabulary from stories they read, this board can be changed to reinforce anything—all the while building reading and writing skills. (You can even use it to teach poetry. See Variations, page 67.) Use it to connect language arts with social studies by listing, for example, places you're studying. Lists and science go together too. If you're studying trees, list species or characteristics. Animals? List baby-animal names—or whatever works with the topic you're investigating.

Building the Board

Steps

1 Cover a bulletin board with paper. Make a heading that says "The List Board."

Materials

- ⊙ craft paper
- ⊙ straight pins
- ⊙ chart paper
- ⊙ pushpins
- ⊙ markers
- ⊙ container

2 Tack up a sheet of chart paper. Use straight pins to put up more than one. When students are ready for a new list, they can just take off the one on top and start fresh.

3 Add a container of markers to the board. (See page 6 for how-to's.)

4 Decide on a list topic, come up with a couple of ideas together, and use them to start the list. Then turn over the board to students. (See Making a List, below, for lots of list ideas.)

MAKING A LIST

Once you begin brainstorming lists to make, you'll find no shortage of ideas. Here's our list of lists you can make. Brainstorm more ideas with students based on what's happening in your classroom.

- ⊙ things I can do (see photo, page 66)
- ⊙ things we want to learn about
- ⊙ characters/events in a story
- ⊙ new words in a story
- ⊙ words we know that start with _____
- ⊙ words we know that rhyme with _____
- ⊙ words for how things feel (*rough, smooth, prickly*, and so on)
- ⊙ synonyms for *nice* (or any other overused word, such as *great*)
- ⊙ places we've been
- ⊙ places we'd like to visit
- ⊙ words that describe a character in a story
- ⊙ words about rain (*wet, drop, puddles, splash*, and so on)
- ⊙ words that describe weather

- ⊙ authors we know
- ⊙ observations of _____ (a science focus)
- ⊙ things that belong in a group (such as fruits, vegetables, things that come in twos)
- ⊙ story ideas

TIP

To add visual appeal to the list, cut out shapes that go with the list (like the stars in the photo on page 66) and place them in a box or envelope on the board. As children add items to the list, have them write their names on the shapes and place them next to their ideas.

Variations

Poetry Place: Use the list board to explore poetry. Begin by reading aloud a "list" poem. "Sound of Water" by Mary O'Neill is a lively example. (See reproducible poem, page 69.) Brainstorm topics for collaborative list poems. Using "Sound of Water" as inspiration, students might create other "sound" poems—"Sound of Night," "Sound of Morning," "Sound of School," and so on.

Start the poem as a group. Post a fresh sheet of chart paper and write a title and the first few words. Let students continue on their own, adding words to the list to continue the poem. Students can make list poems on their own too, then add them to the board.

The sound of rain is
Sprinkling,
Splashing,
Swishing,
Splatting,
Tapping,
Plopping,
Dropping,
Beating,
Pounding,
Drumming.

Teaching With the Board

Lists allow children to read and write in abbreviated forms, making them accessible to everyone—including reluctant readers and writers. They also provide an example of the kinds of reading and writing people do in their daily lives. Suggestions for using lists in your classroom follow:

To Build Self-Esteem: Start the year with a list that gets students off to a positive start—Things I Can Do. Like Things I Can Do, almost any list that invites children to share something about themselves will boost confidence—giving children the message that each of them is important. Things I Like to Do With My Parent(s)/Grandparent(s)/and so on and Something I'm Trying to Learn at Home/School are just a few that will promote positive feelings.

To Reinforce Phonics Skills: Notice sounds that can be reinforced in books you're reading with children. Display a sign that says "Can you find a word that begins with the ____ sound?" Reread the story, letting children take turns adding words to the list. After the story, let children continue to add words from other sources to the list on their own. These words might come from other books, from print material around the room, even their own names.

To Build Process Skills: Use lists with science lessons to strengthen observation and other skills. For example, place a list near a window to encourage observation of the world outside. Invite children to record what they see when they look out the window. Read the list together, noticing word choices (such as words that descibe or compare), details, and so on.

Name _____ Date _____

Sound of Water

The sound of water is:
Rain,
Lap,
Fold,
Slap,
Gurgle,
Splash,
Churn,
Crash,
Murmur,
Pour,
Ripple,
Roar,
Plunge,
Drip,
Spout,
Skip,
Sprinkle,
Flow,
Ice,
Snow.

Mary O'Neill

From WHAT IS THAT SOUND? by Mary O'Neill. Copyright © 1966 by Mary O'Neill. © renewed 1994 Erin Baroni and Abigail Hagler. Reprinted by permission of Marian Reiner.

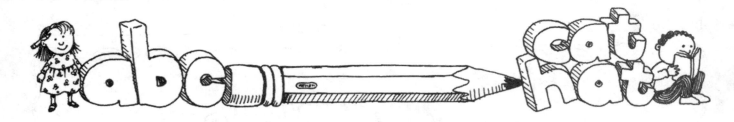

Tell Me How

Children will have fun writing step-by-step directions to build this board. Of course, it's only natural to let them follow their directions to make the real thing—peanut butter and jelly sandwiches (or any other favorite food)!

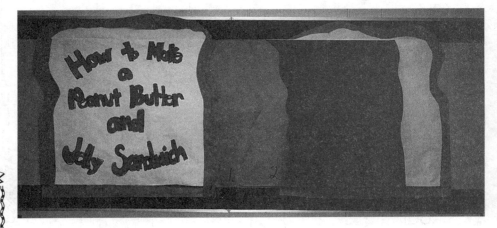

BORDER BOX

The board pictured is borderless. To jazz up your border, have children make paper-doll-like jars of peanut butter and jelly, and then decorate them. (See page 7 for directions.)

LANGUAGE ARTS LINKS

Writing and following directions offers children opportunities for authentic writing (and reading). You can introduce the activity by listing directions people read and write every day. As children go on to write—and then follow—their own directions for making peanut butter and jelly sandwiches, they'll discover the importance of both sequence and detail.

Building the Board

Steps

1 Create the backdrop for your board. The sample pictured above shows white, brown, and red craft paper cut into bread-shaped pieces, then stapled to the board to indicate the layers of a peanut butter and jelly sandwich. To provide additional support for your students, you can number the layers—one for bread, two for peanut butter, three for jelly, four for the second slice of bread. However, you'll get directions more representative of children's thinking if you leave this open.

Materials

- craft paper (white, brown, red or purple)
- construction paper (light brown, white)
- white paper
- scissors
- peanut butter
- jelly
- bread
- plastic knives

2 Ask children to think through the steps for making peanut butter and jelly sandwiches, and then write them on "slices" of bread (paper, cut into bread-size pieces), one step per slice.

3 Have children arrange their slices in order on the board to make peanut butter and jelly sandwiches.

4 Bring out the peanut butter, jelly, and bread and let students follow their directions to make sandwiches. How many end up with the peanut butter and jelly in the middle of two slices of bread?

Teaching With the Board

From labels on food we eat to party invitations, our everyday lives are filled with reasons to read and write. Following are additional ways to incorporate authentic reading and writing into your classroom activities.

More How-To's for Writing: How to make peanut butter and jelly sandwiches is just one set of directions students can write. Brainstorm other directions, such as:

- how to make chocolate milk.
- how to get from the classroom to the cafeteria.
- how to tie your shoes.
- how to get from home to school.

A Recipe Book: Children's ideas about how to make some of their favorite foods make for charming recipe books. Share recipe books and discuss formats for this kind of writing. Then invite children to write and illustrate recipes for their favorite foods, listing ingredients and telling what to do. Make a class set of each recipe, collate, and bind. Let children wrap up recipe books and give as gifts to their families.

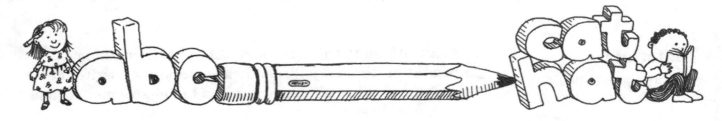

Shoe Shop

Is it a shoe?
No...it's a high-top,
a ballet slipper, a
moccasin, a moon
walker! As
children draw
pictures of
favorite shoes and
label them, they'll
discover that there
are many words
for the things
people put on
their feet!

BORDER BOX

Borders that will work well
for this board include
handprints, student-drawn
faces, and pictures of a
variety of homes.

LANGUAGE ARTS LINKS

This board introduces the concept of using specific language
to express ideas with precision. As children begin to see that
there are many words for *shoe*, they can apply this notion to
their own writing, finding words that, for example, precisely
express how someone is *laughing* (*snickering, chortling, chuck-
ling*) or *walking* (*strutting, marching, tiptoeing*).

Building the Board

Steps

1 Cover a bulletin board with blue craft paper. Cut a slightly smaller piece of white paper and place it over the blue
background. Add a title ("Favorite Shoes") and, if you
like, a giant sneaker or other shoe. Set out a box of markers and crayons on a nearby table, or pin the open box
right to the board. (See page 6.)

Materials

⊙ craft paper (blue, white)
⊙ scissors
⊙ markers
⊙ crayons

2 Invite children to add to the board, drawing pictures of favorite shoes and labeling them.

3 Take time to read the board, noticing all the different words for shoes.

4 Use the board to segue into other activities designed to strengthen word choice. (See Teaching With the Board.) And when children have filled up the board with as many kinds of shoes as they can, start a new board—one that invites children to use specific language to describe desserts or other things. (See Variations.)

Variations °

Board Changers:

Transform your Shoe Shop board by putting up a fresh piece of paper and changing the name. Several suggestions follow:

⊙ **Dessert Shop:** Children add pictures and labels for favorite desserts, such as banana cream pudding or chocolate chunk brownies.

⊙ **Building Board:** Children add pictures and labels for different kinds of buildings, such as pueblo, log cabin, high-rise, and apartment building.

⊙ **Shirt Shop:** Children add pictures and labels to describe shirts they wear—for example, turtleneck, T-shirt, flannel shirt.

⊙ **Rainy Day Descriptions:** Children combine words for different kinds of rainfall with pictures that represent them—for example, drizzle, downpour, and mist.

⊙ **Postage Stamp Shop:** Let children design postage stamps. (You can connect this to curriculum by having them feature, for example, people, events, or places they're studying.)

⊙ **Collection Place:** Let children bring in collections in sandwich bags and write captions telling about them. A small table nearby can hold collections that can't be attached to the board.

Teaching With the Board

From strengthening children's word choices to graphing shoe size, this bulletin board will inspire many curriculum connections. A few suggestions follow:

Fine-Tuning Word Choice: Help children fine-tune their word choices by exploring specific language in a mini-lesson. Write the word *walking* on chart paper. Ask students to think of different ways they walk. Can they creep? (Let them pantomime the word.) Waddle? Saunter? Stroll? Write words for *walk* on the chart paper. Post it for easy reference. Try the same thing to discover specific words for *eat*, *talk*, *move*, and other verbs.

Shoes Make Graphs: Let children use their feet and footwear in a variety of math activities. Start by making a graph to show how many children wear sneakers, shoes, boots, and so on. (Elicit children's help in deciding what categories to graph. For example, they may suggest graphing by high-top/low, laces/no laces, black/not black.) Follow up by graphing by size, again using the actual shoes.

Measuring My Foot: Many children will recall having their feet measured at a shoe store. Explore other ways to measure feet using unifix cubes. Have children trace their feet on paper, and use unifix cubes to measure them. Questions to guide their explorations follow:

- How many cubes fit inside your foot? (They'll be exploring surface area.)
- Will the same number fit inside each foot? (What can children conclude about the sizes of their feet?)
- How many cubes long is the longest part of your foot? (They'll be taking linear measurements.)

Follow up by brainstorming the ways people use measurement in their daily lives—for example, in carpentry work (measuring lengths of wood for building), sewing (measuring fabric to cut), driving (measuring distances), and sports (measuring yards run in football, feet jumped in track and field, and so on). Talk about other kinds of measurement too, such as weight (measuring produce at the market), volume (measuring ingredients for a recipe), and temperature (checking a thermometer to see how warm or cold it is).

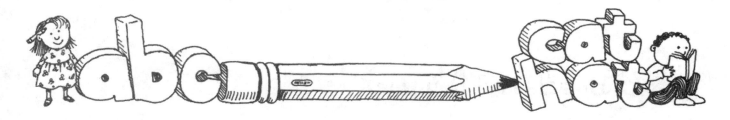

Pick a Pal

This is a student favorite. Pictures of characters from books, taped to dowels, decorate the board. Children can borrow them from the board and take them for walks around the room, reading everything in sight—words on the wall, in books, on boxes, shirts, and bubble gum wrappers. Children can read to the puppets or let the puppets "read" to them!

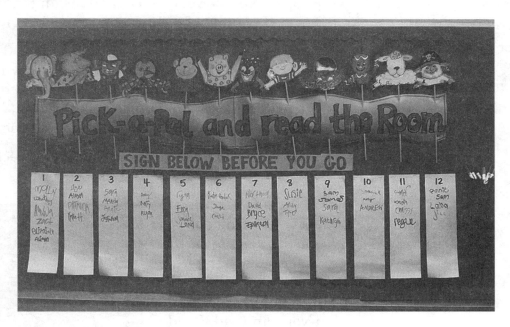

BORDER BOX
The board pictured here has a simple scalloped edge. To customize a border, give children border-width strips of paper and invite them to draw rows of book characters. Put the strips together to make a border for your board.

LANGUAGE ARTS LINKS:

This board encourages children's awareness of the importance and abundance of words in the world around us—not just in books but in many other aspects of life. As they see just how many ways they can "read the room," they'll grow in their appreciation of the many ways reading permeates our everyday lives—for example, game directions, license plates, choices on a menu, signs, words on a computer screen, directions on a bottle of medicine, movie listings, newspapers, and more.

Building the Board

Steps

Materials

- tagboard
- scissors
- markers, crayons
- dowels (cut into 12-inch pieces)
- sturdy tape
- craft paper
- chart paper
- hole punch or glue and Velcro
- holder for markers (see page 6)

1 Invite children to help you create puppets for the board. Begin by brainstorming favorite book characters. Then children can draw pictures of the characters on tagboard, cut around them, and tape them to dowels. Vote on a dozen or so to display on the first board.

2 Cover the board with craft paper. About a foot from the top, add a long sign that reads "Pick a Pal and Read the Room." Below the sign, add a smaller one that says "Sign Below Before You Go."

3 Across the bottom, post strips of chart paper, one strip per puppet. Number each strip and, as an organizational aid, write the name of a character on each strip and tape a tag with the same number to the character.

4 Place puppets on the board. You may, as shown on page 75, punch a series of holes across the top and bottom of the "Pick a Pal" sign and slip dowels through, or glue Velcro to the back of each puppet and to the board.

5 Add a holder for markers. (See page 6 for directions.)

6 Model ways to use the puppets, selecting one, writing your name on the corresponding chart paper, then taking a walk around the room to see what you can read. Read to the puppet or let the puppet read to you or a student.

7 Let children sign their names to the strips when they borrow puppets. Use the strips to monitor the board, noticing who is using the board, how often, which characters are a hit and which aren't, and so on.

Variations ·

Fresh Faces: Keep the board fresh by adding new puppets occasionally. Students can help by preparing puppets ahead of time so that when it's time to add some fresh faces, there are puppets ready to go.

Getting to Know Me: On the back of each puppet, write the name of the book in which the character can be found. Add author and illustrator, too, to familiarize students with a range of reading material.

Keep Reading: Change the sign to read "Pick a Pal and Read the School," "Read the Hall," "Read the Walls," "Read a Story," and so on.

Teaching With the Board

Your read-the-room characters will inspire children to discover many reasons to read.

Reading Roundup: Start a list of reasons to read, and watch it grow. Children can add everything from books to words on shirts and jackets children wear. Continue to explore reasons to read by inviting children to list things people read at home—from newspapers and phone messages to cereal boxes and toothpaste tubes.

Walkabout: Make mini-clipboards with students before heading out for this activity. Cut cardboard into 6- by 8-inch pieces and use paper clips to hold paper in place. Have children take clipboards and pencils and head out with you to read the school. Can they find signs? Names? What other kinds of words fill the hallways? Have children take notes as they go. Compare and compile information.

Reading Pals Materials: Let children and their families discover all the reasons to read at home. Send reading pals home with students, complete with a journal page. (See sample.) Ask children to take their reading pals and family members on a tour of their homes—stopping to notice reading opportunities). Starting in the kitchen, for example, children might find recipes, cereal boxes, shopping lists, notes on the refrigerator, and so on.

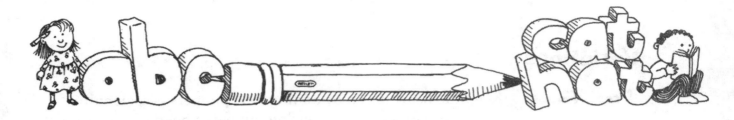

Snapshots

Here are snapshots of a few more favorite interactive language arts bulletin boards to give you a quick look at other ideas. Feel free to adapt what you see—use the photographs and captions to customize boards for your classroom.

All Aboard the Reading Express

"I think I can, I think I can…" is what your students will be saying when they head over to this bulletin board to choose a new reading book. "I thought I could, I thought I could…" is what you'll hear when they finish! Stock the pockets on this board with books you and your students select for independent reading. These might be books that support a theme you're teaching or a more varied selection. You can also include books that students write.

Fun With a Friend

Read this board, sing it, let children count the multiple words. Then let them explore on their own, matching pictures to words, finding endings (-s, -ing, -ed), rhyming words, and so on. Change the board to fit any language arts focus, such as spelling and letter recognition (shown here).

78

You Write It...
We'll Read It!

Start this board with a border and a sign, and your students will do the rest. Clip clothespins (the spring type) to heavy cardboard to make easy clipboards for students to use. Tie on a colorful pen, add a few seats nearby, and watch your young writers fill up the board. You might want to post a list of kinds of writing nearby to inspire students' thinking. Notes, memos, lists, letters, comic strips, plays, and jokes are just a few ideas.

Puzzles on Parade

You can change this board as often as you and your students can make new word puzzles to share. To make a puzzle, draw a picture, write the word for the picture in big letters on the inside, then cut apart to make two or more puzzle pieces, each with one or more letters. Attach pieces of Velcro to the board as well as the backs of the puzzle pieces. Display in random order. Children can play at the board, putting word puzzles together. You'll hear them organizing their plan of attack—saying the names of the letters, sounding out word parts, putting beginnings and endings together until they find words that make sense. Children can also use puzzles they put together to write stories. (Provide chart paper. They can write stories, inserting the pictures rebus-style.) What other ways can students learn at this board? Ask them for a great brainstorming lesson!

Add a Fact

The only thing you do to set up this board is display the topic and add a border. You can use it as a form of a KWL chart, letting students add facts they already know, then including additional information, pictures, and so on as they learn more. Make sticky notes available—students can use them to post a quick fact and to make corrections to previously posted information they want to correct.

Story Wall

This board is easy and inviting. Just hang a few long pieces of white paper and let children add the heading "Story Wall" at the top. Add markers and crayons and let children draw and write freely. Watch to see what emerges. Children might stick to labeling pictures; some might write long, elaborate stories; others might collaborate to write and illustrate stories (one starting the story and others adding on).

Fractured Favorites

This board is fun for friends—two or more children working together to sort and unscramble fairy tales. Have children retell fairy tales on sentence strips (or take dictation from them). Mix up the sentence strips and place them on the board. Let children visit the board, telling the story as they sort the strips. Tip: Space may limit them to retelling an abbreviated version of the story.